An Untried Hand

Publishing without …

CONTENTS …

or

…DISCONTENTS

First:

TRIPPING POINTS

1. Dissection

Look at the cadaver, arranged on its side, as tools take hold. It's oozing wire and screws. So heavy to move, most of the compact frame is vacant, with its sockets, plugs and motherboard clinging to the metal flanks. There's the fan and hard drive, also cooled and lifeless.

For five years, was this the couple's intellect, where the cutest tunes and finest clips were discovered? Were their boldest projects and happier snaps crafted inside?

Or, from its quiet corner, did this box of steel and plastic tilt at the spirit of who they were, like subsidence, or dry rot?

2. Christmas Eve

During the second half of their marriage, fungus had burrowed through the front gardens like moles, perforating the loam, swallowing up privet from its roots and blotting other leaves. He had promised to place bare-rooted plants in the old ones' graves, by Christmas.

Autumn retreated, and his weekday garden was obscured by dusk, like curtains closing to work routines. Weekends were the recovery ward.

He collected the hedging on 23rd December, spending the next morning digging, sifting and chucking the old, while dibbling and firming up the new, in kneaded earth. Finishing by noon, he decided to reduce his dose.

3. Woman's Hour

She chose her last working day because most of her colleagues would be on leave. There was little to do, with the building as pallid and hollow as a husk, and the remaining farewells predictably over-rehearsed or sham-fisted.

Back in the car park, the holly and berberis persisted in piercing the waterlogged bark, while trapping the debris from dizzy drinks and cast off food. Signposts spelt irrelevant names.

As she accelerated past the flagpole and fences, a radio interview began, with someone who'd lost the same sort of job as hers, years before.

He spoke with feeling, through the lies.

4. Death Of A Supermarket

There had been a similar fuss when the Regal cinema was due to close, its legacy the building's silhouette, abrupt and ugly at the crossroads by the church.

Fifty years later, the locals endured the store's systematic demise as they might have gossiped about a retirement, complaining attentively in often unfamiliar aisles.

In the final week, shelves were dismantled in some kind of coded order: booze and bric-a-brac, tins and trolleys, frozen and free range bargains.

By Easter Saturday, a nucleus of chocolate and lunch-stuff remained. The last to visit bought neither, and he wondered at why he'd joined them.

5. Flockless

It was a dry spring fortnight, greening slowly those low motorway meadows, where wheat had been switched for sheep, and the buzzards were spiralling.

Driven to walk by caffeine fever, rather than curiosity, she'd enjoyed crossing the corroded cambers of her previous commute. These led past a telegraph kestrel and the piggery, a cud-bath of cheerful chuntering.

Her husband had insisted on coming, but as they passed the poultry plant, she realised from his chatter that he was neither listening to her, nor noticing the fog-coloured lambs, scattered at their feet.

It might have been a stroll through a whiteout.

6. Tripping Point

It's easy to fall, during rain, but after dark, the mishap provokes its own shadowplays.

First, the scramble for essentials: coins, an unread novel, and those musical leads and phones. There follows a subdued cruise through the hinterlands of snub DIY warehouses and cluttered forecourts, the dial flirting with each new speed sign. Arriving consists of slinking awkwardly past paramedics, whose trolleys and tubes induce feelings of sidelined clumsiness.

Hours later, leaving gains another walk through those neon vistas of near-empty chairs and vending machines, with a support bandage and a prescription of murmured platitudes.

The milkman's hailed at dawn.

7. Chainsaw

The town's hub marked the millennium with some predictable additions to the spokes of its past: creeping precincts; a shuffle of market stalls; the rebranding of buildings, old and new, quaint and awkward.

For years, a facelift was mooted for the broadest street, adding saplings, seating and patterned paving. Work began that March, with a mechanical urgency that thrust at the townsfolk *hi-viz* and hoardings, dust and diversions.

Six weeks later, she parted from the Saturday crowds and paused outside Boots to consider the carcass of a lone tree, felled as it came into leaf, after standing for three decades.

8. Glitterbug

The vial found him in the third week of illness. Pushed to the sill's end, its refracted pattern spattered the gloss. A scrap of paper was wound about the quicksilver contents, with an invitation to scribble a wish.

That was too open-ended, so he woke at dawn and uncorked the magic dust, tipping a trail from bedroom to landing, hall to lounge. Draughts pushed splinters to the skirts and jambs.

Inevitably, his wife swept and sucked away most of the grains of his fantasy. Weeks later, she explained why, but by then he was wishing that it would all disappear.

9. Lapwings

She discovered the lane in early spring, when the merging fields were free of blossom, leaf or crop. Their furrows spooled out in most directions, meeting hawthorn, undrained hollows or undergrowth in the gundog woods.

Once, she watched four lapwings dipping and wheeling above an untilled stretch at the lane's end, their flight as jagged as their sharp, synthetic cries.

On May Day, she was stalled at the same point by the frenetic call of one such bird, hovering at about four metres. Beyond, a black tractor trawled the stubble, turning dead ground and newly-laid eggs to a tumbling flood.

10. A Mosaical Map

With its condensed settings and textures, his district was as large and various as the Isle of Wight. In the varying fractions of what he had left, he marshalled the shards of memory by setting out somehow to walk each of the borough's footpaths.

Neither propelled by particular method or melancholy, he spread across the loft floor each photograph from these wanderings, watching them glimmer and grow into a schema that sprawled over side roads and sluices, pastures, paddocks and plantations.

Nearing completion, his montage spent more and more time in the dark, those steps steepening, as the card curled.

11. Long Off

She loved the local cricket ground, but hated the game, and would plan any foray to avoid the summer matches. Winter and week day strolls began on a rutted track to the lop-sided gates, brushing under cherry trees and past the brick, mock-Tudor pavilion.

One Tuesday in early July, she diverted to the sedate cul-de-sac where that turf plateau had been nurtured for as far back as she could recall. But a full game was unfolding - a vulgar bleaching of the field.

The charade was affirmed as a lanky youth sauntered towards the stumps, locks flailing.

Another called, "Well bowled, Chloe!"

12. Too Close To Heaven

He remembered how this small corner of countryside had affected him: the tractors' growl, a couple of crops away; starlings abroad, and the city skyline of angular flats and industry, as blunt as turrets. Such views.

He'd admired how this public by-way had been allowed to merge with the drive, skirting a lawn that revealed how labourers' cottages had been sculpted into a large home.

Now a fence and gate prevailed, the latter displaying a sign: 'Beware of the Geese'.

Overhead, honking migrants lamented the spirit of a place that he'd avoided since the separation of their friends, years before.

13. Moving In

The pigeon down drifting across the lawn proved that a raptor had been there, as elusive as the young tawny owl, that screeched after dusk from lampposts and leylandii.

Not always so. On no particular afternoon, she was drawn to the back yard by the insistent calls of nesting blackbirds, one hedge down. A sparrow hawk straddled the privet, talons grasping the splintered remains of a pigeon, while the male blackbird darted from branch to branch of the evergreen undergrowth.

And those mustard-bright eyes looked through her, and across the lawns and fruit trees, towards the next feed.

We've been watched.

14. After Autumn

By mid-October, most of the garden's floral swatch card had paled to sallow leaves or sepia stumps. The final folds of sedum and African daisy preserved some shades of crimson and magenta, which flashed when the afternoon sun found a way through.

Pollen-seekers had been sprinkled across the previous week, butterflies skittering between bees, for a few hours. Skippers and fritillaries gave the bolder brush strokes, peacocks and red admirals the finer features.

He hadn't spoken to her for days, and wondered at these jarring colours, as living leaves parted from the wings of those that were about to vanish.

Then:

ARRIVING AT ISLANDS

Mooring

At anchor
        he's rolling beside her as he sleeps,
before the final dial falls limp
and   the   crew   set   to
with their mopped up lists
                    and electric chores.

At anchor
        she leaves the dull wheel hut adrift
and checks her tablet's later tales,
as   the   hull's   low   breath
lets the shore nuzzle up
                to sigh and swell.

At anchor
        she rides out sleep, wishing he would wake,
his hull held to the saline cleft
where   the   urgent   shoals
reflect how he might
                rise again with her.

Rhum

'It's a graveyard, really...'

                                        grabbing our gaze
                                 as the bow turns hard
                                   past the black house,
                                  sharp at the old quay
                          where windfalls of yachts
                                        turn like tides,
                                         closing cloud.

'Scan the loch
and your old snaps,
to see where you were:
we're berthing briefly...

                                                 'It's needless,
                                an island of vacancies,
                                     the wooded crofts
                                       for strayabouts
                                    and eco-exiles,
                                    dark and gravelled,
                                      up their squat
                                  and unnamed lanes.

                                     Thirty years since,
                                  the phone box groans.
                              No one staffs the castle.

'You were as lost
in your callow age,
way back then...'

                                      given these hills
                                        for a week
                                    before wedding,
                                  hauling the sitka
                                      past tree lines,
                                  to shove in the bog.

'There's your plantation:
wrong conifers, though.
They poison the soil'.

Raasay

*'Don't you know of the route
that he built with a spade
and a barrow? Well, here goes.*

*That Calum was the last
at Arnish, crofter, postie,
Rona's keeper, picking
a scrap with Inverness
and the hills and burns,
to take ten years to shape
and scrape a homeward road...'*

> But he opened it up
> to a closing township,
> émigrés skipping
> his twisting life-lane
> through the marsh.

*'Two hours, once
we've beached up the dingy.
Should be enough...'*

> Did Calum guess
> he'd connected a wasteland?
> Did he die
> blistered, but happy?
> Today, as we're
> enclosed by sleet,
> peaks erase
> and the bay contracts,
> but Arnish breathes
> past the road's end.
> Clans of cars
> face contract-cabins,
> holiday crofts,
> a pebble-dashed slipway
> and, under the turbines,
> signs for free range swine.

*'Good walk? You see,
I warned you it was laid too late...'*

Inverie, Loch Nevis

Pictured to death,
these mainland isles,
give dangerously,
their village and hamlet
staring us in:
Our Lady in plastic arcs
- storms orbit.

> *'That's where we were,*
> *last May, with friends,*
> *delivered by outboard,*
> *in cartons and fibre glass.*
> *Great walks and weather,*
> *You can't imagine…'*

By August, this melting light
lugs out each day
to the loch's mouth,
reaching westward
past high water murk
and farmstead shambles.

> *'But better was dragging*
> *the folklore*
> *from local lairds:*
> *one impresario,*
> *another explorer,*
> *both so unspoilt*
> *in their quirky piles.*
> *Their retainers*
> *treated us like kings…'*

Post-dusk, we hang
off the stern,
scanning the log
from porpoise to eagle.
Cottages hold to the shore
like floats for a net
that's under, around and beyond
this tin of minnows.

Skye, Isleornsay

Fifteen conning towers.

Or, these torpedoes –
muscled missiles -
have our measure,
taped, and in their sights.

> *'Why's he turning?*
> *Dolphins! DOLPHINS!*
> *left of the quayside.*
> *where's my tripod?'*

Steeled to our steel,
they hug the hull
and spill their clicks
across the radar -
propelling propellers,
harbouring harbours.

> *'They're under us,*
> *and tracking the bow,*
> *so near we can trace*
> *each scar and lesion...'*

Which kinds of seadog
surround our boat:
some skittish pups,
wet off the leash
and safe from the depths?
a pod of collies,
that tagged and tugs us
into this ring of stone?
or packs of jackals,
yelping threats
and daring us to take them on?

> *'Look*
> *at the youngster,*
> *eying us up,*
> *each time he leaps.*
> *What a show off...'*

After that:

AN UNTRUE HAND

```
The Quakers' graveyard names the lane,  slabs and captions
over-                                                 lost
sown                                                  once
with                      a                          rooks
pine,                   noose                         told
turf,                   droops                        more
moss,                                                 than
then                                                  rite,
preserved by a date in its bricks, when the plague raged.
```

```
                        Once
              a                an
           gifted           untanned
         jeweller's             gap
          flicker           appeared
           linked              forty
           youth              years'
            to                 bond
          lineage    Signet    lost
           that              sloppily
            odd              leaving
          heraldic           exposed
           bauble              this
          arming              worn
            an                 and
              untried   untrue
                       hand
```

> **PLEASE leave
> this parking
> space for me.
> I live here**

          Do you?

                        Did you?

        Stalking home

                           last light

    we shot a glimpse

                        curtains forlorn

   closing themselves

                            overworn coat

hung up to die

                              an empty smell

his photos, shamed

                          the standard damp

lazy paving

                             undead heads

     manicured thorn

                      and water ruts.

        Wonder weather

                 storm shrouds

            bore him

           out...

S I R E n   s I R E N

breeze-black clouds   great grey roofs

          crops of crows   gangs of gulls

scratched tracks   fat paths

SCREAM   or   BAWL

                      and

                                             this

terrace-
       flashed
                                                         gutter-
                                                ground

                   blaring
     gap-
                                  dodgem-
                                      drilled

wail-
       wiped
                                                    harried-
                                              howl

       bloody
                                                          scar

                   tears
                             up

~~runts of villages~~
                                                    ~~squabbled~~
                                                 ~~streets~~

Market day stalwarts

ambled
        and bustled
                and chivvied
                        and dawdled
                                and edged
taking stock of stacks of stock   and flitted
like stock cars, stuck at the start.

On days like those

I've glided,
      you've hustled
           he's inched
                she's jostled
                      we've keeled
over the odds   and they've limped
for oddballs' nods and bends.

On days like these

I mosey
      you nip
           she outstrips
                he prowls
from car to bar   we queue
to barter, barring bargains.   and they rumble

Days will fall

when we'll sidle
      or traipse
           unseat
                vamoose
as fast as whoever   or wiggle,
we're ageing to be,   and expire
- blank or enraged and fit   to yield
                                        or zoom.

Commuting (In Reverse)

Through the smear of a window
facing backwards
jackdaws argue in the Astro's goal
p e e l i n g off
like a buddleia branch line

| Fed by |

that signal box once, at the halt
with its vistas of turbines and waterlogged hawthorn

where lambs skedaddle from frost

which floods the glass house hives

by dyke or sluice or tributary

and poplar parallelograms

& pulling in, the arms of a Priory arch

hide by a shrubbery.

Formby Point

Two summers   on the move.

The Latitude tide,

where surf-seekers

mustered by sand-winds

take to the trudge

their bootload of sea-dreams

in plastic and flash tones,

divvied across

a strandful of paths

magnified

pointing west to the waves.

The Longitude swells

from asparagus pens

to Nicotine Wood

and anorak gangs

shoot up red rodents

or comb the inshore

for recent fossils

magnetised

by the marram surge,

needles and cones.

Thanks to the editors of these journals and enterprises where versions and selections of these poems have appeared, or been short or longlisted, or commended: MMU's *Avis*; Coast to Coast to Coast Pamphlets 2018; *Envoi*; Loughborough University's Overton Competition; *mgversion2>datura*; EHU's *Mothmaw*.

© *Will Daunt 2021*

This is number 7 of a limited edition of 10 copies.

ISBN: 9781794855229

£4

Other adventures:

Lancashire Working
Running Out Of England
The Good Is Abroad
Distant Close
Powerless
Landed
Town Fliers/ Town Criers
Thousands Bourn
England's Edging, Parts One & Two
Every Dark Advance

Gerard Manley Hopkins: the Lydiate Connections

Edited adventures:

Tim Noble: *Writing On Rock*
Eddie Wainwright: *Pleading At The Bar Of Truth*
P.E. Daunt: *Ten Letters To A Grandson*